ᑎᒻᒥᐊᑦ ᐱᐊᕋᖕᒋᓪᓗ
TINGMIAT PIARANGILLU
ADULT AND BABY BIRDS

ᑎᑎᖅᑐᒐᖅᑐᖅ

ᐃᒪ ᐲᑐᓴᓐ

TITIQTUGAQTUQ ILLUSTRATED BY

Emma Pedersen

ᐅᓇ ᐅᒃᐱᒡᔪᐊᖅ.

Una ukpigjuaq.

This is a snowy owl.

ᐅᓇ ᐅᒃᐹᕋᖅ.

Una ukpaaraq.

This is a snowy owlet.

ᐅᓇ ᑲᖑᖅ.

Una kanguq.

This is a snow goose.

ᐅᓇ ᑲᖑᐊᕋᖅ.

Una kanguaraq.

This is a snow gosling.

ᐅᓇ ᖁᐸᓄᐊᖅ.

Una qupanuaq.

This is a snow bunting.

ᐅᓇ ᐊᐃᑦᑕᐅᓵᖅ.

Una aittausaaq.

This is a snow bunting chick.